Look! Listen! Think!

Grades 2-3

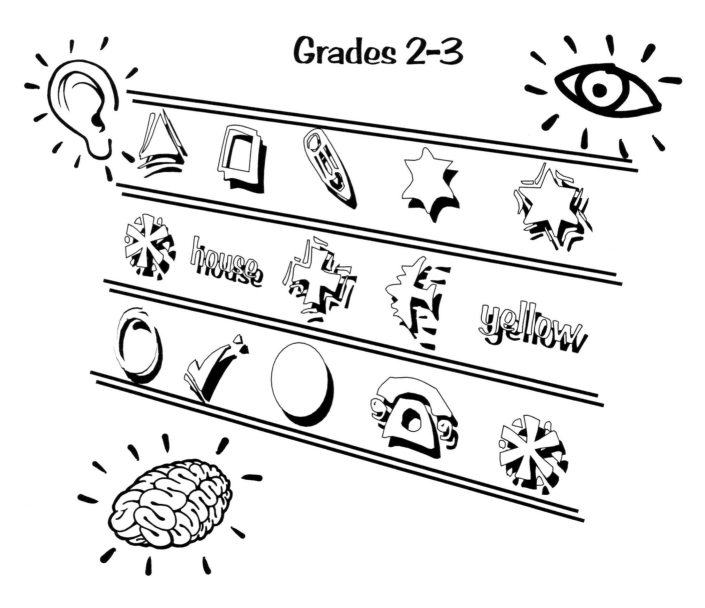

Written By Jean Edwards

Published By World Teachers Press®

Order Number 2-5094
ISBN 978-1-58324-016-8

H I J K L 11 10 09 08 07

395 Main Street
Rowley, MA 01969
www.didax.com

Foreword ◀▮▮▮

Look! Listen! Think! is a series of three books designed to provide you with activities to exercise the minds of your students.

Each book contains a series of developmental activities in the following areas:

(i) Visual discrimination and memory skills—being able to remember what they have seen and answer questions accordingly; and

(ii) Listening comprehension and memory skills—being able to remember what they have heard and follow oral instructions correctly.

Both sections provide you with detailed information to ensure the procedures are easy to follow and administer. Sections can be tackled in any order, but the activities within each section gradually become more difficult, so should be used from set one through to the final set.

Contents ◀▮▮▮

Teacher Information...

...Visual Memory Skills ⬅⫷

- Distribute picture to students. It may be cut off separately or the question side may be folded back.

- Students study picture for a time you specify. (Suggestion – 60 seconds for grades two and three.)

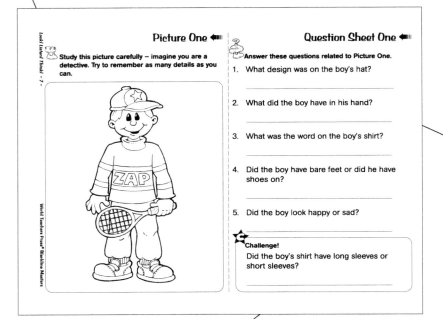

Picture One ⬅⫷

Study this picture carefully – imagine you are a detective. Try to remember as many details as you can.

ZAP

Question Sheet One ⬅⫷

Answer these questions related to Picture One.

1. What design was on the boy's hat?

2. What did the boy have in his hand?

3. What was the word on the boy's shirt?

4. Did the boy have bare feet or did he have shoes on?

5. Did the boy look happy or sad?

Challenge!
Did the boy's shirt have long sleeves or short sleeves?

- Picture is turned over.

- Students answer questions. You may read the questions if there are reading difficulties.

- Activity may also be given verbally on an individual basis with you writing the responses.

- Challenge! is answered but not recorded on scoring sheet.

- Distribute a scoring sheet from page 18 to each student.

- Scores can be recorded by:

  (a) students individually checking the picture;

  (b) teacher marking individually; or

  (c) teacher discussing answers with the whole class.

- Do not ask the students to call out their score unless they are comfortable with this approach.

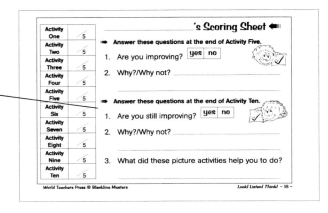

Activity One	/5
Activity Two	/5
Activity Three	/5
Activity Four	/5
Activity Five	/5
Activity Six	/5
Activity Seven	/5
Activity Eight	/5
Activity Nine	/5
Activity Ten	/5

's Scoring Sheet ⬅⫷

➡ Answer these questions at the end of Activity Five.

1. Are you improving? yes no

2. Why?/Why not? _____

➡ Answer these questions at the end of Activity Ten.

1. Are you still improving? yes no

2. Why?/Why not? _____

3. What did these picture activities help you to do?

Teacher Information...

...Listening Memory Skills ◄▐▐▐

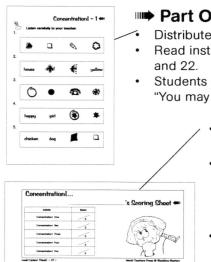

▐▐▐► Part One – Concentration!

- Distribute student activity page.
- Read instructions from teacher copy on pages 21 and 22.
- Students complete each row after you say, "You may begin."

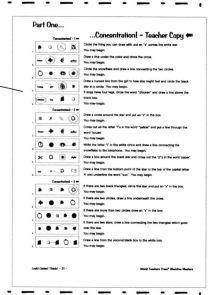

- Distribute a scoring sheet from page 28 to each student.
- Scores can be recorded by:
  - (a) teacher marking individually; or
  - (b) teacher discussing answers with the whole class.
- Do not ask students to call out their score unless they are comfortable with this approach.

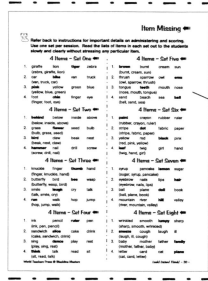

▐▐▐► Part Two – Item Missing

- Distribute a scoring sheet from page 32 to each student.

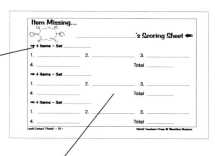

- Administer "Item Missing" activities to students from pages 30 and 31.

- Student writes missing item on scoring sheet.
- Supply the answers and students record their score.
- Do not ask students to call out their score unless they are comfortable with this approach.

▐▐▐► Parts Three and Four – Digits Forwards and Digits Backwards

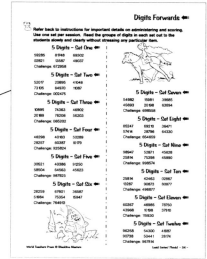

- Distribute a scoring sheet from page 36 or 40 to each student.
- Administer the "Digits Forwards" activities from pages 34 and 35, and "Digits Backwards" activities from pages 38 and 39.
- Student writes the sequence of digits on the scoring sheet whether it be forwards or backwards.

- Supply the answers and students record their score.
- Do not ask students to call out their score unless they are comfortable with this approach.
- Challenge! is answered on the sheet but not recorded in the total.

Visual Memory Skills

Visual discrimination and visual memory skills form an integral part of many daily activities. They are essential and critical skill areas, but we don't often, or regularly, teach or consciously develop them in our classroom program.

Visual discrimination and visual memory skills can be enhanced by practice and your students will benefit from regular exercises at least once a week. These activities will help to provide that practice.

You can explain to your students that the mind is rather like a muscle, in that it can be exercised and strengthened and that these activities are designed to provide that exercise.

The illustrations on the following pages are to help improve visual discrimination and visual memory skills. The activities become gradually more difficult.

The pages have been designed to be used in two ways.
1. You can cut the page down the middle and distribute the picture. The students turn the illustration over after studying it and you read the questions.

2. The students fold the page down the middle and study the picture side. Then they turn it over to answer the questions without being able to see the picture. Be sure the students do not read the questions before studying the picture.

In this section students are required to remember what they have seen in the picture and answer questions accordingly.

Instructions

⟶ Tell the students that the activity is to help them with their visual memory—remembering details of what they have seen. (Like playing detective.)

⟶ Distribute a copy of the illustration to each student and allow them a stated time to scan the illustration; for example, sixty seconds for students in grades two and three.

⟶ Turn the illustration over and answer the questions on the answer sheet—this allows students to work at their own pace.

⟶ You can also read the questions, allowing suitable time for answering if there are reading difficulties.

⟶ The activity can also be given verbally on an individual basis, with you writing the student's responses.

Scoring

⟶ Students can mark their own work, by checking the illustration, or you can discuss the answers with the students.

⟶ Students enter their score on the scoring sheet provided on page 18.

Question Sheet One

Answer these questions related to Picture One.

1. What design was on the boy's hat?
   _____

2. What did the boy have in his hand?
   _____

3. What was the word on the boy's shirt?
   _____

4. Did the boy have bare feet or did he have shoes on?
   _____

5. Did the boy look happy or sad?
   _____

Challenge!

Did the boy's shirt have long sleeves or short sleeves?
   _____

Picture One

Study this picture carefully—imagine you are a detective. Try to remember as many details as you can.

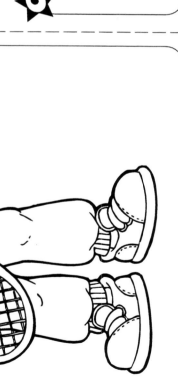

Question Sheet Two

Answer these questions related to Picture Two.

1. What color was the girl's hair?

2. What did she have on her feet?

3. How many buttons were on her blouse?

4. What was in her right hand?

5. What design was on her shorts?

Challenge!

Did the girl have a collar on her blouse?

Picture Two

Study this picture carefully—imagine you are a detective. Try to remember as many details as you can.

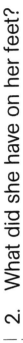

Question Sheet Three

Answer these questions related to Picture Three.

1. How many cushions was the girl leaning against? _____

2. What was the girl doing? _____

3. What was the picture on the wall showing? _____

4. Could you see the nail holding up the picture? _____

5. Did the girl have ribbons in her hair? _____

Challenge!

Which foot was on top of the other? _____

Picture Three

Study this picture carefully—imagine you are a detective. Try to remember as many details as you can.

Question Sheet Four

Answer these questions related to Picture Four.

1. What was the boy doing?

   _____

2. How many felt pens were lying on top of the desk?

   _____

3. Was the boy left- or right-handed?

   _____

4. What was the boy doing with the hand that wasn't holding the felt pen?

   _____

5. Name the other item on the desk besides the paper and felt pens.

   _____

Challenge!

How many little lines were marked on the ruler in the picture?

_____

Picture Four

Study this picture carefully–imagine you are a detective. Try to remember as many details as you can.

Question Sheet Five

Answer these questions related to Picture Five.

1. How many pillows could you see on the bed?

2. Were the numbers on the clock in black or white?

3. How many books were on the bedside table?

4. Could you see one of the boy's ears?

5. How many knobs could you see on the bedside drawer?

Challenge!
Could you see the teddy's mouth above the bedclothes?

Picture Five

Study this picture carefully—imagine you are a detective. Try to remember as many details as you can.

Answer these questions related to Picture Six.

1. Could you see both the girl's ears?

2. Was the girl's hair tucked behind her ears?

3. How many cars were right side up?

4. Did the girl have bare feet?

5. Was the girl wearing shorts?

✦ **Challenge!**

Imagine you are the girl. Which hand was touching the top of the car?

Picture Six ◀▥

Study this picture carefully—imagine you are a detective. Try to remember as many details as you can.

Question Sheet Seven

Answer these questions related to Picture Seven.

1. Which hand was the lady holding the hammer in?

2. Was the lady on flat feet or tiptoes?

3. How many nails were lying on the floor?

4. Was there an electric outlet on the wall?

5. Did the jar on the floor have a lid?

Challenge!

How many flowers were in the vase in the picture?

Picture Seven

Study this picture carefully—imagine you are a detective. Try to remember as many details as you can.

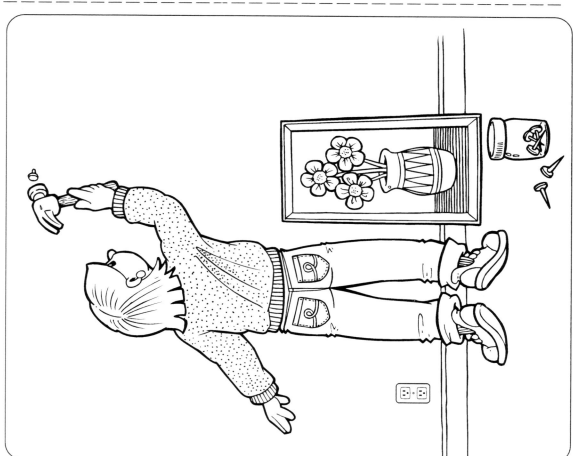

Question Sheet Eight

Answer these questions related to Picture Eight.

1. How many buttons were on the girl's overalls?

   _____

2. What was the boy holding in his left hand?

   _____

3. How many toys were on the floor?

   _____

4. What was the dog doing?

   _____

5. What was the pattern on the boy's shorts?

   _____

Challenge!

What was the picture on the jigsaw puzzle?

   _____

Picture Eight

Study this picture carefully—imagine you are a detective. Try to remember as many details as you can.

Question Sheet Nine

Answer these questions related to Picture Nine.

1. How many apples were on the table?

2. What was the time on the clock?

3. Was the baby happy or sad?

4. Which hand was the girl using to eat her cereal?

5. What was Mom cooking for breakfast?

Challenge!

How many flowers were in the vase?

Picture Nine

Study this picture carefully—imagine you are a detective. Try to remember as many details as you can.

Question Sheet Ten

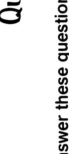

Answer these questions related to Picture Ten.

1. How many monkeys were in the tree?

_____

2. What was the elephant doing?

_____

3. How many people were wearing a hat?

_____

4. Was anybody wearing shorts?

_____

5. Could you see both tusks on the elephant?

_____

Challenge!

How many people were taking photographs?

Picture Ten

Study this picture carefully—imagine you are a detective. Try to remember as many details as you can.

Answers...

Picture One – Page 7

1. star
2. racquet
3. Zap
4. shoes
5. happy
☆ long

Picture Two – Page 8

1. black
2. thongs/sandals
3. three
4. fishing rod
5. spots/dots
☆ yes

Picture Three – Page 9

1. one
2. reading
3. lady
4. yes
5. yes
☆ left foot

Picture Four – Page 10

1. drawing
2. three
3. right-handed
4. holding his head
5. ruler
☆ six

Picture Five – Page 11

1. two
2. white
3. three
4. yes
5. one
☆ yes

Picture Six – Page 12

1. yes
2. yes
3. four
4. no
5. no
☆ right hand

Picture Seven – Page 13

1. right hand
2. tiptoes
3. two
4. two
5. yes
☆ three

Picture Eight – Page 14

1. two
2. nothing
3. three
4. sleeping
5. stripes
☆ clown

Picture Nine – Page 15

1. three
2. 7 o'clock
3. sad
4. right hand
5. toast
☆ one

Picture Ten – Page 16

1. two
2. squirting water
3. four
4. yes
5. no
☆ one

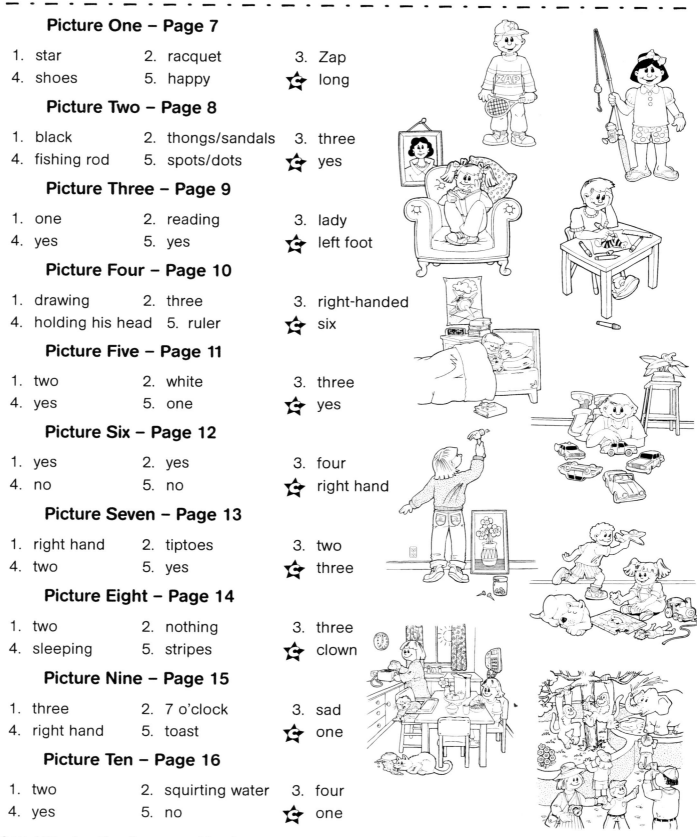

Activity One	/ 5
Activity Two	/ 5
Activity Three	/ 5
Activity Four	/ 5
Activity Five	/ 5
Activity Six	/ 5
Activity Seven	/ 5
Activity Eight	/ 5
Activity Nine	/ 5
Activity Ten	/ 5

_____ 's **Scoring Sheet** ◀‖‖

▪▶ **Answer these questions at the end of Activity Five.**

1. Are you improving? | yes | no |

2. Why?/Why not? _____

_____

▪▶ **Answer these questions at the end of Activity Ten.**

1. Are you still improving? | yes | no |

2. Why?/Why not? _____

_____

3. What did these picture activities help you to do?

_____

Activity One	/ 5
Activity Two	/ 5
Activity Three	/ 5
Activity Four	/ 5
Activity Five	/ 5
Activity Six	/ 5
Activity Seven	/ 5
Activity Eight	/ 5
Activity Nine	/ 5
Activity Ten	/ 5

_____ 's **Scoring Sheet** ◀‖‖

▪▶ **Answer these questions at the end of Activity Five.**

1. Are you improving? | yes | no |

2. Why?/Why not? _____

_____

▪▶ **Answer these questions at the end of Activity Ten.**

1. Are you still improving? | yes | no |

2. Why?/Why not? _____

_____

3. What did these picture activities help you to do?

Listening Memory Skills

Listening and memory skills form an integral part of many daily activities, such as reading, spelling, writing and mathematics.

They are essential and critical skill areas that are not often isolated for specific development and attention in our classroom programs.

Listening and memory skills can be enhanced by practice, and your students will benefit from regular exercises at least once a week. These activities will help to provide that practice. They are structured to provide your students with practice in auditory memory, auditory discrimination, memory and concentration skills.

You can explain to your students that the mind is rather like a muscle, in that it can be exercised and strengthened and that these activities are designed to provide that exercise.

The activities in this section are divided into the following subsections:

➠   Concentration!—*listening, concentration and memory*

➠   Item Missing—*listening and memory*

➠   Digits Forwards—*listening and memory*

➠   Digits Backwards—*listening, concentration and memory*

The subsections may be used in any order, however, the sequences within each subsection are in ascending order of difficulty and it is recommended that you follow them through in their entirety.

Part One...

...Concentration! ◀||||

In this section, students are required to listen carefully to oral instructions and complete the activity.

The *Concentration!* activities in this section gradually become more complex. Therefore, it is suggested that you work through the activities in the order they are presented. The activities are designed to develop listening, concentration and memory skills with an emphasis on concentration.

Instructions

⟫ Tell the students that this activity is designed to help them practice and sharpen their concentration skills. You are going to read a sentence telling them things they can do with each row of pictures or symbols, so they need to listen carefully. You will not be repeating any of the instructions, so they need to listen and concentrate as best they can.

⟫ Tell the students that you are going to do the whole page, one row at a time.

⟫ Ask them not to make any noise or ask any questions once you have begun, otherwise, they might distract someone else who is trying hard to concentrate.

⟫ Tell the students that you are going to read the instructions for each row of symbols. The students are to listen and refrain from working until they hear you say, "You may begin."

⟫ Once you have finished giving the instructions, the students then try to remember what you have said and do their work on their activity sheet. Stress that students are not to begin working until you have said, "You may begin."
NOTE: Tell your students that if they copy the work of others here, they are defeating only themselves as they won't be training themselves to be better listeners. Being honest with themselves here sets them up for success with more difficult sets in the future.

⟫ When you are ready to begin, read aloud each instruction slowly, deliberately and clearly. Give the students ample time to complete each row before moving on to the next. Use one activity sheet per session. The activity has been copied twice on the page to reduce the amount of photocopying you need to do.

Scoring

⟫ Use the answers on the *Teacher Copy* (pages 21 and 22) to correct the students' work. Record scores on the scoring sheet on page 28.

⟫ NOTE: The scoring sheets are designed so students can monitor their own individual progress—they are not designed to compare scores with anyone else. Please avoid asking the students to call their scores aloud in front of the class unless the students say they are quite comfortable with this. You may collect totals individually instead.

Part One...

...Concentration! – Teacher Copy ◀▥

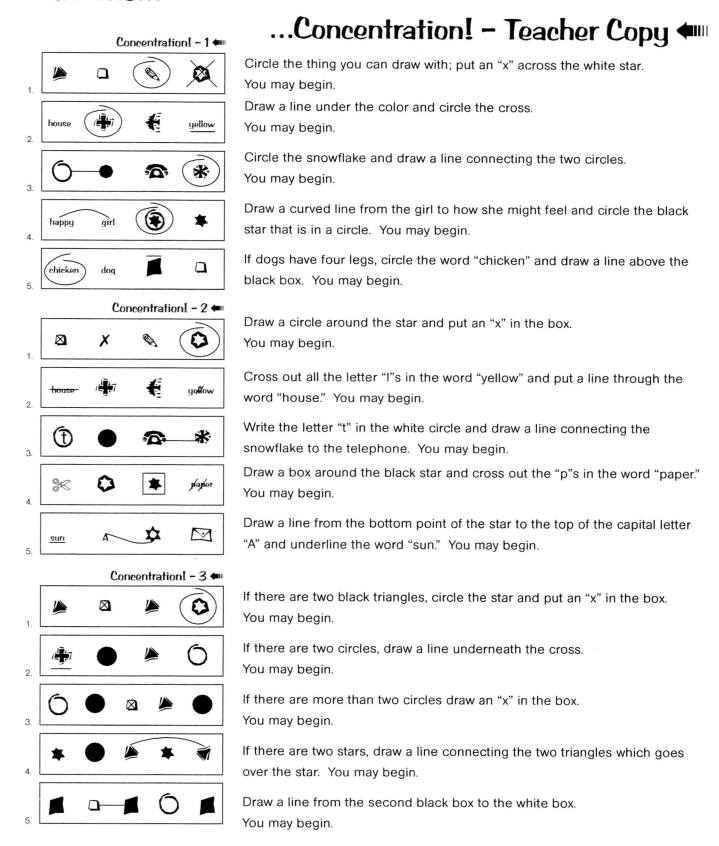

Concentration! – 1 ◀▥

Circle the thing you can draw with; put an "x" across the white star.
You may begin.

Draw a line under the color and circle the cross.
You may begin.

Circle the snowflake and draw a line connecting the two circles.
You may begin.

Draw a curved line from the girl to how she might feel and circle the black star that is in a circle. You may begin.

If dogs have four legs, circle the word "chicken" and draw a line above the black box. You may begin.

Concentration! – 2 ◀▥

Draw a circle around the star and put an "x" in the box.
You may begin.

Cross out all the letter "l"s in the word "yellow" and put a line through the word "house." You may begin.

Write the letter "t" in the white circle and draw a line connecting the snowflake to the telephone. You may begin.

Draw a box around the black star and cross out the "p"s in the word "paper."
You may begin.

Draw a line from the bottom point of the star to the top of the capital letter "A" and underline the word "sun." You may begin.

Concentration! – 3 ◀▥

If there are two black triangles, circle the star and put an "x" in the box.
You may begin.

If there are two circles, draw a line underneath the cross.
You may begin.

If there are more than two circles draw an "x" in the box.
You may begin.

If there are two stars, draw a line connecting the two triangles which goes over the star. You may begin.

Draw a line from the second black box to the white box.
You may begin.

Part One...

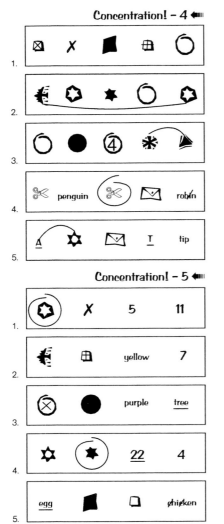

Put a cross in the second white box and an "x" in the first one.
You may begin.

Draw a line from the plane to the second white star.
You may begin.

Put a number four in the second white circle and draw a line connecting the top of the snowflake to the top point of the triangle. You may begin.

Cross out the "i" in the bird that can fly and circle the second pair of scissors. You may begin.

Draw a line from the top of the capital letter "A" to the top point of the star and if there are two capital letters in this row, put a line under each of them. You may begin.

If there are two numbers and one is less than ten, circle the star.
You may begin.

If there is a number less than five, circle the plane and if there is a number larger than five put a cross in the box. You may begin.

If there is something that grows, underline it, if there are two circles put an "x" in the first circle. You may begin.

Underline the largest number and if there is an even number, circle the black star. You may begin.

Cross out all the "c"s in the word "chicken" and if there are two boxes, underline the word "egg." You may begin.

Concentration! – 1 ◄▐▐▐

Listen carefully to your teacher.

1. 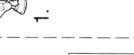 □ ✏️ ✡️

2. house ✠ 🦇 yellow

3. ⬭ ⬤ 🚗 ❋

4. happy girl ⍟ ★

5. chicken dog ◼ □

Concentration! – 1 ◄▐▐▐

Listen carefully to your teacher.

1.  □ ✏️ ✡️

2. house ✠ 🦇 yellow

3. ⬭ ⬤ 🚗 ❋

4. happy girl ⍟ ★

5. chicken dog ◼ □

© World Teachers Press® – www.worldteacherspress.com

Look! Listen! Think! – 23 –

Listen carefully to your teacher.

1.

2. house   yellow

3.

4. paper   scissors

5. sun   A

Concentration! – 2

Listen carefully to your teacher.

1.

2. house   yellow

3.

4. paper   scissors

5. sun   A

Listen carefully to your teacher.

1.
2.
3.
4.
5.

Concentration! – 3

Listen carefully to your teacher.

1.
2.
3.
4.
5.

Look! Listen! Think! – 25 –

Concentration! – 4

Listen carefully to your teacher.

1.

2.

3.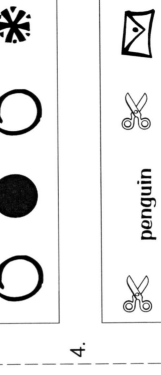

4. penguin   robin

5. A   T   tip

Concentration! – 4

Listen carefully to your teacher.

1.

2.

3.

4. penguin   robin

5. A   T   tip

Listen carefully to your teacher.

1. | ✡ | ✕ | 5 | 11 |

2. | 🦇 | ⬜ | yellow | 7 |

3. | ◯ | ⬤ | purple | tree |

4. | ✡ | ★ | 22 | 4 |

5. | egg | ◼ | ⬜ | chicken |

Concentration! – 5

Listen carefully to your teacher.

1. | ✡ | ✕ | 5 | 11 |

2. | 🦇 | ⬜ | yellow | 7 |

3. | ◯ | ⬤ | purple | tree |

4. | ✡ | ★ | 22 | 4 |

5. | egg | ◼ | ⬜ | chicken |

Concentration!...

_____'s Scoring Sheet ◀║║║

Activity	Score
Concentration! One	5
Concentration! Two	5
Concentration! Three	5
Concentration! Four	5
Concentration! Five	5

Concentration!...

_____'s Scoring Sheet ◀║║║

Activity	Score
Concentration! One	5
Concentration! Two	5
Concentration! Three	5
Concentration! Four	5
Concentration! Five	5

Concentration!...

_____'s Scoring Sheet ◀║║║

Activity	Score
Concentration! One	5
Concentration! Two	5
Concentration! Three	5
Concentration! Four	5
Concentration! Five	5

Part Two...

In this section, students are required to listen carefully to two lists of items read by the teacher. They then write the missing item from the second list.

The *Item Missing* activities gradually become more complex. Therefore, it is suggested that you work through the sets of activities in the order they are presented. The activities are designed to develop listening and memory skills.

Instructions

▶ Discuss the fact that exercising or training the mind is similar to training a muscle... success will not be instantaneous, it takes regular practice.

▶ Use one set of *Item Missing* activities per session. Read both the initial list and the set in brackets, which has one item missing. Read them aloud to the students, slowly, deliberately and clearly, without stressing any particular item. The missing item in each list is in bold type.

▶ Once you have finished giving each list of items, the students then write the missing item on the scoring sheet on page 32. Give your students time to ponder.

Scoring

▶ Read the complete set again and supply the answer. Record scores on the scoring sheet on page 32.

▶ Tell your students that you expect them to be honest—they will be cheating only themselves if, for instance, they score their work incorrectly.

▶ By filling out their scoring sheets students will be able to monitor their progress, hopefully seeing the improvements they are making when they total their scores each month, assuming you are doing one set each week.

▶ If improvements are not being made, go back a level and give further practice until the student is ready to move on to a more advanced level.

▶ NOTE: The scoring sheets are designed so students can monitor their own individual progress—they are not designed to compare scores with anyone else. Please avoid asking the students to call their scores aloud in front of the class unless the students say they are quite comfortable with this. You may collect totals individually instead.

Refer back to instructions for important details on administering and scoring. Use one set per session. Read the lists of items in each set to the students slowly and clearly without stressing any particular item.

3 Items – Set One

1. **cat**   horse   dog
   (horse, dog)
2. car   **van**   truck
   (truck, car)
3. **cake**   candy   cookie
   (cookie, candy)
4. finger   eye   **foot**
   (finger, eye)
5. hop   **skip**   jump
   (jump, hop)

3 Items – Set Two

1. word   **book**   paper
   (paper, word)
2. grass   **sun**   bulb
   (bulb, grass)
3. bird   beak   **nest**
   (beak, bird)
4. nail   **hammer**   screw
   (nail, screw)
5. purple   **red**   black
   (black, purple)

3 Items – Set Three

1. **cup**   saucer   knife
   (saucer, knife)
2. **sky**   sea   bird
   (sea, bird)
3. mouth   **hair**   eyes
   (eyes, mouth)
4. **bed**   chair   napkin
   (napkin, chair)
5. shoe   bird   **fly**
   (bird, shoe)

3 Items – Set Four

1. thick   **thin**   enormous
   (enormous, thick)
2. round   square   **oblong**
   (round, square)
3. hedge   **tree**   bush
   (bush, hedge)
4. giraffe   **lion**   tiger
   (tiger, giraffe)
5. **kiwi**   koala   kangaroo
   (kangaroo, koala)

3 Items – Set Five

1. true   **funny**   lie
   (lie, true)
2. **waves**   foam   seaweed
   (foam, seaweed)
3. **shell**   crab   mussel
   (mussel, crab)
4. bread   cake   **tea**
   (cake, bread)
5. **card**   present   birthday
   (present, birthday)

3 Items – Set Six

1. scratch   shake   **rub**
   (shake, scratch)
2. **Mary**   George   Tom
   (George, Tom)
3. doctor   **driver**   nurse
   (nurse, doctor)
4. **store**   road   house
   (house, road)
5. ribbon   **bow**   brush
   (ribbon, brush)

Refer back to instructions for important details on administering and scoring. Use one set per session. Read the lists of items in each set to the students slowly and clearly without stressing any particular item.

4 Items – Set One ⬅||||

1. giraffe   lion   **tiger**   zebra
   (zebra, giraffe, lion)
2. car   **bike**   van   truck
   (van, truck, car)
3. **pink**   yellow   green   blue
   (yellow, blue, green)
4. foot   **chin**   finger   eye
   (finger, foot, eye)

4 Items – Set Two ⬅||||

1. **behind**   below   inside   above
   (below, inside, above)
2. grass   **flower**   seed   bulb
   (bulb, grass, seed)
3. **bird**   claw   beak   nest
   (beak, nest, claw)
4. **hammer**   nail   drill   screw
   (screw, drill, nail)

4 Items – Set Three ⬅||||

1. knuckle   finger   **thumb**   hand
   (finger, knuckle, hand)
2. butterfly   bird   **bee**   wasp
   (butterfly, wasp, bird)
3. smile   **laugh**   cry   talk
   (talk, smile, cry)
4. **run**   walk   hop   jump
   (hop, jump, walk)

4 Items – Set Four ⬅||||

1. ink   pencil   **ruler**   pen
   (ink, pen, pencil)
2. sandwich   **slice**   cake   drink
   (cake, sandwich, drink)
3. sing   **dance**   play   rest
   (play, sing, rest)
4. **think**   talk   read   sit
   (sit, read, talk)

4 Items – Set Five ⬅||||

1. **brown**   burned   cream   sun
   (burned, cream, sun)
2. thrush   sparrow   owl   **robin**
   (owl, sparrow, thrush)
3. tongue   **teeth**   mouth   nose
   (nose, mouth, tongue)
4. sand   beach   sea   **ball**
   (sand, sea, beach)

4 Items – Set Six ⬅||||

1. **paint**   crayon   rubber   ruler
   (rubber, crayon, ruler)
2. stripe   **dot**   fabric   paper
   (stripe, fabric, paper)
3. yellow   red   **black**   pink
   (red, pink, yellow)
4. **leaf**   twig   girl   hand
   (twig, hand, girl)

4 Items – Set Seven ⬅||||

1. syrup   pancake   **lemon**   sugar
   (sugar, syrup, pancake)
2. eyebrow   nails   lips   **hair**
   (eyebrow, nails, lips)
3. ball   plane   **doll**   book
   (ball, plane, book)
4. mountain   river   **hill**   valley
   (river, mountain, valley)

4 Items – Set Eight ⬅||||

1. wrinkled   smooth   **lumpy**   sharp
   (sharp, smooth, wrinkled)
2. **sneeze**   cough   laugh   ill
   (laugh, ill, cough)
3. baby   mother   father   **family**
   (mother, father, baby)
4. letter   card   cat   **plane**
   (cat, card, letter)

Item Missing...

_____ 's Scoring Sheet ⬅||||

▶ **3 Items – Set** _____

1. _____ 2. _____ 3. _____

4. _____ 5. _____ Total _____

▶ **3 Items – Set** _____

1. _____ 2. _____ 3. _____

4. _____ 5. _____ Total _____

▶ **3 Items – Set** _____

1. _____ 2. _____ 3. _____

4. _____ 5. _____ Total _____

- -

Item Missing...

_____ 's Scoring Sheet ⬅||||

▶ **4 Items – Set** _____

1. _____ 2. _____ 3. _____

4. _____   Total _____

▶ **4 Items – Set** _____

1. _____ 2. _____ 3. _____

4. _____   Total _____

▶ **4 Items – Set** _____

1. _____ 2. _____ 3. _____

4. _____   Total _____

Part Three...

In this section, students are required to listen to a group of digits read by the teacher. They write the same sequence of digits from memory.

Instructions

⏩ Discuss the fact that exercising or training the mind is somewhat similar to training a muscle... success will not be instantaneous, it takes regular practice.

⏩ Use one set of *Digits Forwards* activities per session. Read one group of digits at a time aloud to the students, slowly and clearly, without stressing any particular digit.

⏩ Once you have finished reading each group of digits, the students then write the same sequence of digits from memory on their scoring sheet. Stress that students are to refrain from writing until you have finished reading the group aloud. Give the students time to ponder. Repeat with each group of digits until the set is complete.

⏩ A "challenge" from the next level is enjoyed by most students and one is provided for each set.

Scoring

⏩ Read each group of digits in the set for students to check their answers. Use the scoring sheet on page 36 to record individual scores. The "challenge" is not recorded in the total on the scoring sheet—this is purely to help develop self-confidence.

⏩ Tell your students that you expect them to be honest with themselves—they will be cheating only themselves if they score their work incorrectly, or begin to write the number before being told.

⏩ By filling out their scoring sheets students will be able to monitor their progress and hopefully see the improvements they are making when they total their scores each month, assuming you are doing these each week.

⏩ If improvements are not being made, go back a level and give further practice until the student is ready to move on to a more advanced level.

⏩ NOTE: The scoring sheet on page 36 is designed so students can monitor their own individual progress—they are not designed to compare scores with anyone else. Please avoid asking the students to call their scores aloud in front of the class, unless the students say they are quite comfortable with this. You may collect totals individually instead.

Refer back to instructions for important details on administering and scoring. Use one set per session. Read the groups of digits in each set to the students slowly and clearly without stressing any particular item.

4 Digits – Set One ⬅|||

4793	8659	4602
5871	6107	1073

Challenge: 72958

4 Digits – Set Two ⬅|||

8385	2249	7184
9482	4428	5027

Challenge: 20975

4 Digits – Set Three ⬅|||

0896	5746	2810
1954	3756	7913

Challenge: 49358

4 Digits – Set Four ⬅|||

9755	6784	2807
3935	5714	6467

Challenge: 20871

4 Digits – Set Five ⬅|||

1905	5791	3964
2087	4962	1073

Challenge: 69084

4 Digits – Set Six ⬅|||

5747	9027	8543
2091	6897	9170

Challenge: 67054

4 Digits – Set Seven ⬅|||

3726	5467	9012
8098	2312	4352

Challenge: 13476

4 Digits – Set Eight ⬅|||

9087	4587	3450
6523	1896	7654

Challenge: 90873

4 Digits – Set Nine ⬅|||

4432	8761	0987
3861	6036	4159

Challenge: 35098

4 Digits – Set Ten ⬅|||

5567	9812	9641
7652	3958	1753

Challenge: 39082

4 Digits – Set Eleven ⬅|||

8904	6752	4432
8863	2348	5319

Challenge: 89468

4 Digits – Set Twelve ⬅|||

5278	9423	8734
9741	2749	6709

Challenge: 59083

Refer back to instructions for important details on administering and scoring. Use one set per session. Read the groups of digits in each set to the students slowly and clearly without stressing any particular item.

5 Digits – Set One ←||||

59285	81748	69302
02821	13587	49037

Challenge: 672958

5 Digits – Set Two ←||||

52017	20895	41048
73105	64970	11087

Challenge: 002475

5 Digits – Set Three ←||||

10895	74363	46902
20189	76208	56203

Challenge: 085202

5 Digits – Set Four ←||||

46298	40183	50289
28257	60387	10179

Challenge: 925824

5 Digits – Set Five ←||||

30521	40386	91250
58504	64563	45623

Challenge: 987925

5 Digits – Set Six ←||||

28259	67601	36587
51984	75354	15947

Challenge: 764913

5 Digits – Set Seven ←||||

54982	15981	39685
45693	20198	63694

Challenge: 698558

5 Digits – Set Eight ←||||

85247	69210	36471
57414	28796	64330

Challenge: 654659

5 Digits – Set Nine ←||||

98947	52871	45628
25814	75398	45890

Challenge: 998574

5 Digits – Set Ten ←||||

25814	42463	02867
13287	90873	80977

Challenge: 496877

5 Digits – Set Eleven ←||||

60357	46985	78750
43968	10198	37910

Challenge: 115930

5 Digits – Set Twelve ←||||

96358	54300	41987
90738	50441	28174

Challenge: 967814

Digits Forwards...

_____'s Scoring Sheet ⬅

➡ **4 Digits – Set** _____

_____ _____ _____ _____ _____

_____ Challenge _____ Total _____

➡ **4 Digits – Set** _____

_____ _____ _____ _____ _____

_____ Challenge _____ Total _____

➡ **4 Digits – Set** _____

_____ _____ _____ _____ _____

_____ Challenge _____ Total _____

Digits Forwards...

_____'s Scoring Sheet ⬅

➡ **5 Digits – Set** _____

_____ _____ _____ _____ _____

_____ Challenge _____ Total _____

➡ **5 Digits – Set** _____

_____ _____ _____ _____ _____

_____ Challenge _____ Total _____

➡ **5 Digits – Set** _____

_____ _____ _____ _____ _____

_____ Challenge _____ Total _____

Part Four...

...Digits Backwards ◀‖‖‖

In this section, students are required to listen to a group of digits read by the teacher. They write the same sequence of digits from memory in reverse order.

Instructions

▮▶ Use one set of *Digits Backwards* activities per session. Read one group of digits at a time aloud to the students slowly and clearly, without stressing any particular digit.

▮▶ Once you have finished reading each group of digits, the students then write the same sequence of digits from memory on their scoring sheet in reverse order. Stress that the students are to refrain from writing until you have finished reading the group aloud.

▮▶ Students should not write the digits down from right to left on their page, or write them from left to right and then rewrite them reversed; but should hold the sequence in their memory and turn it around. For example, if the sequence given is 456, they should remember it, turn it around and write 654.

▮▶ It should be stressed to the students that they are training their minds, in essence, to memorize and manipulate items. If they don't hold the sequence in their minds and turn it around before writing it down, they are not training themselves for subsequent sets. Honesty here sets them up for more difficult future sets. Honesty is the best policy.

▮▶ A "challenge" from the next level is enjoyed by most students and one is provided for each set.

Scoring

▮▶ Read each group of digits in reverse order for students to check their answers. Use the scoring sheet on page 40 to record individual scores. The "challenge" is not recorded in the total on the scoring sheet—this is purely to help develop self-confidence.

▮▶ By filling out their scoring sheets students will be able to monitor their progress and hopefully see the improvements they are making when they total their scores each month, assuming you are doing these each week.

▮▶ If improvements are not being made, go back a level and give further practice until the student is ready to move on to a more advanced level.

▮▶ NOTE: The scoring sheet on page 40 is designed so students can monitor their own individual progress—they are not designed to compare scores with anyone else. Please avoid asking the students to call their scores aloud in front of the class, unless the students say they are quite comfortable with this. You may collect totals individually instead.

Refer back to instructions for important details on administering and scoring. Use one set per session. Read the groups of digits in each set to the students slowly and clearly without stressing any particular item.

3 Digits – Set One ←||||

493	597	517
201	826	497

Challenge: 4690

3 Digits – Set Two ←||||

693	571	919
408	583	613

Challenge: 2548

3 Digits – Set Three ←||||

936	571	904
513	384	976

Challenge: 0381

3 Digits – Set Four ←||||

142	983	259
284	510	637

Challenge: 1087

3 Digits – Set Five ←||||

159	634	197
208	157	395

Challenge: 5876

3 Digits – Set Six ←||||

975	595	470
318	847	981

Challenge: 3637

3 Digits – Set Seven ←||||

678	908	321
765	397	194

Challenge: 4180

3 Digits – Set Eight ←||||

961	046	872
931	951	295

Challenge: 7250

3 Digits – Set Nine ←||||

936	294	034
927	620	783

Challenge: 9367

3 Digits – Set Ten ←||||

826	725	763
936	623	961

Challenge: 9071

3 Digits – Set Eleven ←||||

519	542	816
926	062	731

Challenge: 8409

3 Digits – Set Twelve ←||||

310	496	931
624	319	834

Challenge: 0937

Refer back to instructions for important details on administering and scoring. Use one set per session. Read the groups of digits in each set to the students slowly and clearly without stressing any particular item.

4 Digits – Set One ⬅️‖‖

5968	8901	2526
1065	5891	3027

Challenge: 57546

4 Digits – Set Two ⬅️‖‖

1894	5953	1874
2046	6879	3235

Challenge: 10176

4 Digits – Set Three ⬅️‖‖

6923	4628	5981
2859	5980	1579

Challenge: 85981

4 Digits – Set Four ⬅️‖‖

4690	2589	1493
2591	4529	4390

Challenge: 46921

4 Digits – Set Five ⬅️‖‖

6328	2593	1537
4857	1021	0983

Challenge: 46902

4 Digits – Set Six ⬅️‖‖

2981	4690	1527
4258	6250	1302

Challenge: 79213

4 Digits – Set Seven ⬅️‖‖

5942	7881	3507
8024	6237	2094

Challenge: 84281

4 Digits – Set Eight ⬅️‖‖

9731	5579	1579
0979	3574	1597

Challenge: 98734

4 Digits – Set Nine ⬅️‖‖

4983	4982	1320
6754	2798	1127

Challenge: 89710

4 Digits – Set Ten ⬅️‖‖

4697	5670	5749
0389	4218	4615

Challenge: 05974

4 Digits – Set Eleven ⬅️‖‖

4897	5989	5045
8475	4581	1067

Challenge: 36384

4 Digits – Set Twelve ⬅️‖‖

5871	6305	4810
7415	1257	5794

Challenge: 75014

Digits Backwards...

_____'s Scoring Sheet ⬅||||

➨ **3 Digits – Set** _____

_____ _____ _____ _____

_____ Challenge _____ Total _____

➨ **3 Digits – Set** _____

_____ _____ _____ _____

_____ Challenge _____ Total _____

➨ **3 Digits – Set** _____

_____ _____ _____ _____

_____ Challenge _____ Total _____

Digits Backwards...

_____'s Scoring Sheet ⬅||||

➨ **4 Digits – Set** _____

_____ _____ _____ _____

_____ Challenge _____ Total _____

➨ **4 Digits – Set** _____

_____ _____ _____ _____

_____ Challenge _____ Total _____

➨ **4 Digits – Set** _____

_____ _____ _____ _____

_____ Challenge _____ Total _____